Under-hedge Dapple

Janet Philo

Under-hedge Dapple

Janet Philo

Three Drops Press
Sheffield, England

Three Drops Press
Sheffield, United Kingdom

www.threedropspoetry.co.uk

ISBN 978-1-907375-08-8

Three Drops Press is an independent imprint of Endaxi Press.

Cover design and Green Man illustration © Kim McDermottroe 2016

Book layout design © Kate Garrett 2016

Praise for Under-hedge Dapple

"From first sight of the contents page, I knew I was in for a poetic treat. Janet's poems are full of gorgeous alliteration and sibilance, singing in wonderful wordplay. Under-hedge Dapple will leave you basking in a world of dream-like, mystical magic."
– Jane Burn, Founder of *The Fat Damsel*, poet & illustrator

"Like genius and madness, there's a fine line between whimsy and wonder. Janet walks that line effortlessly, serving, at times, an unadulterated sweetness that would be twee in the wrong hands. There's a strong sense of the mythic running through this collection, even when describing the, sometimes, harsh beauty of the North East coast, a place she's obviously connected with. If you like your poems to be joyous, lacking in bland sarcasm and able to evoke joy, and a real sense of wonder and place, then this is for you."
– p.a. morbid, editor of *The Black Light Engine Room*

"These poems seem to come from a faerie realm - not the spun-sugar world of bubblegum-pink Disney fairies, but the thorny, mysterious and dangerously enchanting world of the Old Folk. They are shot through with tangible images of nature from the tiniest thyme flower to the Arctic ice sheets, and everywhere they are as richly colourful as cathedral windows. A real sensual pleasure."
– Kirsten Luckins, Programme Coordinator Apples and Snakes (North)

To Philip, for being there, unfailingly.

Autumn Alchemy

Windfall apples;
silver slices clean
through sweet-stinking,
brown thumb-sinking,
cider-breath decay.
A green-gloss mackintosh
wraps firm flesh,
for one moment more,
before
the rot sets in.

Beetroot's wrinkled robe slips off;
inside she shimmers,
all heart.
Her blood pools purple,
like the blackberry's
perfidious smile,
undulating with
curves of crawling worms.
Their juice laden load
implodes in mouths
of joshing fools,
sucking sticky fingers and
taking summer home,
before the devil spits
amethyst frost and
speckles indigo sloes,
as sweet Ruby Alchemy
weaves her winter dreams.

Cloud Woman

He cannot reach her eyes or know her mind;
he wants her softness, given not coerced,
and stretches fingers, but touch is declined.
As she drifts out of reach, all form dispersed,
pricked by the heat of him, she drips through air;
her eyes are arctic-calved and polished bright
with tears that roll through empty space; white hair
snow-drifts from her, like pinstripes in his night.
He learned the price of dreams on wheels of flame;
he found no joy in woman's human flaws;
mist woman never calls her lover's name.
Liminal life alone behind closed doors;
inside his mind he makes a lost mist maiden;
his life remains outside the fragrant garden.

*Inspired by Ixion, a mortal who tried to seduce Hera, wife of
Zeus. Zeus tempted Ixion with a cloud woman in the shape of
Hera, then punished his transgression with eternal torment on
a wheel of fire.*

After Swim Directions

Look right:
dog-rose-petal morning
blooms
above a cold, rolled-steel
grey sea.

Look ahead:
and breathe,
tide rises in the nostrils;
sea-scented moisture
wrapped in wrack
and the contents of
a mermaid's purse
drenches
this morning in
palest grey,
tipped with white light.

Look left:
marshmallow mist
stretches and yawns;
its grey-whale jaws
filter feed on colour;
mist devours
lines,
inhales
shape

and swallows
yellow,
until a haunting of
turbine trunks
hovers
useless
windless
still.

The Green Man

The Green Man feels.
The Green Man sees.
The Green Man hears
the silent sadness
of the polystyrene Madonna's
cold rolling tears.
Her plea for the green
drips into damp blackness;
the black hole of his ear,
moist with the autumn,
sucking in summer,
listening with foreboding
to the last soft sounds
of the fading year.
Fungus stubble framing
lightly chiselled chin,
asserting masculinity,
promising fecundity
with sleek bracken fronds,
dripping green lifelines
of androgynous beauty,
through summer dry tresses
of sparse tawny grasses.
Face framed,
he listens.
The Green Man feels.
The Green Man sees.
The Green Man hears
the silent sadness
of the polystyrene Madonna's
cold rolling tears.

Woman with Pounamu Chisel

(after working with New Zealand Maori greenstone carver)

Moss-green,
pristine and river-ripped;
milky smudges drift,
like clouds,
towards the whetted tip.
Polish with your sweat,
he says. The chisel
slides like ice-melt
across her salty forehead,
sponges her essence;
shell-cases the pearl in her...
She works in quietness,
keeps his sacred space,
creeps awestruck
through his time,
hammocked
in unbroken threads
of human life.
Suddenly, she reels
alone.
His face now inked with
rage;
tattooed lines
are scars of
ancient tapu
now transgressed.
His mystery fragmented
in one untimely touch...
He calls down summer darkness
and she is lost.
For her,
the thread is cut.
Yet, smoothing,
stroking, working,

warming the stone,
is soothing.
She limps home, scarred,
to daylight,
grips her sweat-stained heirloom.
Her life now gilds the chisel
ingrained in cloud and green.

Pounamu: New Zealand Maori for greenstone
tapu: New Zealand Maori for that put into the sphere of the
sacred, set apart, forbidden and exclusive. The violation of
tapu must result in retribution.

Falling into Green

(after Pollock)

Another me fell,
out of control,
into briars and blood
and blackberry stains,
printing red nettle weals
onto floral chintz skin
in patterns of pain.

Another me fell
under cool bracken curls
to the earth-scented world
of autumn-crunch cushions
as rioting rainbows
dissolved into green.

Another me fell,
like raindrops on garlic;
I touched the white,
I tasted the green.
Rising again with the sun
and the warming
freshly soaked oxygen
kisses the skin.

Another me falls
into green dreams
on a sprung bed of thyme
with a camomile cushion

cradled in green.

Redcar Beach

February frost
pours from the nostrils
of Arctic white horses
tethered at the tideline,
broken on the sand.

Sea Fret

Sea fret
stashes summer
in deep down pockets
of seagull soft grey.
She hears muffled cries
as seabirds glide.
All else is silent,
and she is alone.

Sea fret
drenches kisses,
whispers to skin
of sun glazed blue
that will come again.
For now, out of reach,
and belonging to others.
This rolling grey monster
has stolen her colour.

Sea fret
blots summer,
sucks in the sparkle,
and pockets the gold.
Her hair, for a moment,
drips with spider web
diamonds.
The fret peddles magic, then
slinks off with her dreams...

But fret gives permission
to retreat from the crowd,
from the time,
from the place,
to wrap herself softly,
to stand in her space.

A Poet Torn

(after William Blake's Los)

Sink or spring upwards? Brace, brace, brace!
Lungs squeezed and emptied of innocent song:
a silent scream on a flame frozen face.
Experience burns the heat tortured tongue,
awesome beasts charred in orange and black,
sun warmed gardens now sickened with blight.
Worms curl, petal-cupped; the rose dies back,
while the fire pit churns with a hellish light.
You crave the view from the far away rock
but anchor lines weaken, then all is lost.
You search for starlight in velvet black
where pale sunlight cools to eternal frost.
You hear the message as the comet sings
but fear the frailty of Icarus' wings.

*In the mythological writings of William Blake, Los is the fallen
(earthly or human) form of Urthona, one of the four Zoas. Los
is regularly described as a smith, beating with his hammer on
a forge, which is metaphorically connected to the beating of
the human heart. (Wikipedia)*

Under-hedge Dapple

Faeries live
behind leaf fans
in under-hedge dapple.
They smash
surface tension
on dew drop
perfection,
in sturdy green boots,
psyched-up for contact,
with silver-wired seax
prepped for the piercing,
still blackthorn-buckled
and tucked
at a waist
wrapped
in dark leather
stripped
from the bodice
of a crane fly's babe.
Until...
heavy with clods,
they bask
with the slow worm
on fleeting-warm rock.

Sloe-eyed and watchful,
they wait
for the sun spots
to scatter their wings with
shot-silk iridescence
stolen from nymphs,
while the dragonfly sleeps.
Like crystal-tailed comets
they rocket
through sunlight,
climb spider-built bridges

to the hearts of wild lilies,
where the lord and his lady
patiently wait.

Seax: Anglo Saxon short-bladed knife

Winter Solstice

Some souls die on dark days,
when ice-cool starlight
dips its bleached-bone fingers
in the wind-blown scum of
winter's dirty linen sky,
washed out to palest grey.
Here is just light enough to stir
warm hearts to life:
to wait, and watch
the winking of the candle's eye.

Crossing Teesmouth

She dreams
a rainbow of mackerel,
roping South Gare to North,
where seals steal the silver
mistaking fishermen's lines
for the mackerel's flash:
stomachs full of hooks
lures and condoms
and the broken head of
a toothless brush.

A pyre of burning tyres
sends smoke rings chaining
across the river mouth.
The tide's tongue
plays power games,
as the dirty old rock star,
licking and leering,
drops heavy-metal
on the rim of Paddy's Hole.

Turbines, like stilt walkers,
stride to Seaton from Redcar;
yellow from lemon tops
drips on their boots.
Their coats
hang on mist hooks;
empty,
like razor shells,
pecked out by sea birds
on South Gare sands.

Indian Summer

She first saw a turban
at grandma's door;
she was nut-brown then.
Twig-girl stared wide-eyed
at a scuffed cardboard
suitcase,
straining at straps and
bursting with dreams -
sequins and beads;
snake heads and silks;
ebony elephants walked
gold ribbon-roads
till they poured from the case
down to brown dust
on a sinister shoe
wedged in the door.

Woman is the Spiral Weaver

(After Louise Bourgeois)

Freaky giant spiders
are mother-weavers,
spinning spiral webs and
mapping spirit journeys.
A Tantalus stretch
to reach
her drop down sanity;
climb her Silk Road,
from chaos to captivity.
She clings to hairpin bends
held fast by
inescapable ancestry
and a parallel
mythical past,
woven by women,
from genital hair.
Never alone I
do, undo, redo...
Eight legged contradictions:
repetition and
metamorphosis,
weaving
tangles and loops
into double helix spirals
down which
she slides to
spider stillness.

Samhain Song

Pumpkins, candles, torches, hats...
peep out from your blanket when the
moonlight shines from the eyes of cats.

Owls' eyes, your eyes, my eyes –
round.
hiding, giggling, kicking
leaves along the ground.

Pumpkins, candles, torches, hats...
peep out from your blanket when the
moonlight shines from the eyes of cats.

Charcoal shadows etched on the ground –
leaves crunch – we munch;
sticky-pocket bravery
given and found.

Pumpkins, candles, torches, hats...
peep out from your blanket when the
moonlight shines from the eyes of cats.

Moonlight, starlight,
ice-white fright.
No monsters here,
but hold
hands tight.

Pumpkins, candles, torches, hats...
peep out from your blanket when the
moonlight shines from the eyes of cats.

Safe home shivering,
chocolate sipping,
lost in stories, kiss goodnight...

Pumpkins, candles, torches, hats...
peep out from your blanket when the
moonlight shines from the eyes of cats.

Stopped Clocks

She tried to climb inside a summer's day;
it was a day still enough to stop a dandelion clock.

Yet California Poppies trembled with a mermaid's breath,
sighing in from the sea.

A barbed wire fence of bumble bee buzz
kept her out of the blackbird's nest.

The sun, behind a milky veil of stratus cloud, grilled
cheek bones; sweat dripped from the bridge of her nose,

She remained outside.

Sunday with the Moon

I kneel beside you to converse with the moon.
Shoe polish smudges its face, in lunar eclipse,
while your breath is my clarity, as you sleep-slip and slide
to the darkness of beaches, where slow Sunday ebbs
and your Monday crouches on taut-hamstring haunches,
balled fist at the ready to hammer on our door.

Acknowledgements

Andy Willoughby, Poet and Senior Lecturer in Creative
Writing at Teesside University;
for shining a light on poetry for me.

Kirstin Luckins at Apples and Snakes Ltd, with the Tees
Women Poets; for friendship, support and a generous
sharing of writerly skills and talent.

p.a. morbid at Black Light Engine Room Literary Magazine;
for keeping poetry live in Middlesbrough, and giving new
voices a chance.

Cover Art and Green Man illustration: Thank you so much,
Kim McDermottroe at Greener Lavelle.
www.facebook.com/greenerlavelle

Previous Publication Credits

'Sunday with the Moon' first appeared on *The Fat Damsel,*
Take Ten, Issue 8.

2016 Titles from Three Drops Press

Constellations by Susan Castillo Street
Under-hedge Dapple by Janet Philo
Back to Yesterday by Zöe Broome
There is an island by Johnny Giles
Follow the Stag and Learn to Fly by Anna Percy
The Unicornskin Drum by Stella Bahin
A Sprig of Rowan by Rebecca Gethin
The Darkling Child and Other Stories
         by Catherine Blackfeather
Among the White Roots by Bethany W Pope
The First Greek Tragedy by Cora Greenhill
Lykke and the Nightbird by A.B. Cooper

*Full Moon & Foxglove: An Anthology of Witches
         and Witchcraft* edited by Kate Garrett
Tailfins & Sealskins: An Anthology of Water Lore
         edited by Kate Garrett & Amy Kinsman

www.ingramcontent.com/pod-product-compliance
Lightning Source LLC
Chambersburg PA
CBHW060553030426
42337CB00019B/3537